Acknowledgement of Land & of the Traditional Owners of this Land

I would like to acknowledge the Gadigal people of the Eora Nation, upon whose stolen land I stand on today.
I recognise that this land was never terra nullius — the land belonging to these peoples was never ceded, given up, bought or sold.
I would like to pay my respects to Aboriginal Elders past, present and emerging, and I extend this acknowledgement to all Aboriginal and Torres Strait Islander people.

Blowin` In The Wind

"How many roads must a man walk down
Before you call him a man?
How many seas must a white dove sail
Before she sleeps in the sand?
Yes, and how many times must the cannonballs fly
Before they're forever banned?

The answer, my friend, is blowin' in the wind
The answer is blowin' in the wind.

Yes, and how many years must a mountain exist
Before it is washed to the sea?
And how many years can some people exist
Before they're allowed to be free?
Yes, and how many times can a man turn his head
And pretend that he just doesn't see?

The answer, my friend, is blowin' in the wind
The answer is blowin' in the wind.

Yes, and how many times must a man look up
Before he can see the sky?
And how many ears must one man have
Before he can hear people cry?
Yes, and how many deaths will it take 'til he knows
That too many people have died?

The answer, my friend, is blowin' in the wind
The answer is blowin' in the wind."

Songwriter: Bob Dylan

"Cornucopia"
(Quilt)
By Mariclaire Pringle

Contents

1: Am I Normal?
(Sono Normale?)
2: He Has No Clue What's Going On
(Non ha Idea di cosa stia Succedendo)
3: What Does it All Mean, Mr Jones?
(Cosa Significa tutto questo, Signor Jones?)
4: You're Killing Me with Music
(Mi stai Uccidendo con la Musica)
5: Life is Not a Competition
(Non è una Competizione)
6: Die Before You Die
(Muori Prima di Morire)
7: Your Protector
(Il tuo Protettore)
8: The Establishment
(L'istituzione)
9: Power Corrupts
(Corruzioni di Potere)
10: The Ego
(L'ego)
11: No One Else Can See You Like I See You
(Nessun Altro Può Vederti Come ti Vedo Io)
12: I Am Weak
(Io Sono Debole)
13: I Am a Looney
(Io Sono un Pazzo)
14: I'm Bad
(Io Sono Cattivo)
15: Hidden in the Darkness
(Nascosto nell'Oscurità)
16: We Are All the Same
(Siamo Tutti Uguali)
17: Our Mind
(La Nostra Mente)

Contents

18: Jealousy
(Gelosia)
19: La Luna
(The Moon)
20: Access Denied
(Accesso Negato)
21: Look on the Bright Side of Death
(Guarda il Lato Positivo della Morte)
22: How Does One Grow Old?
(Come Si Invecchia?)
23: Future Man v2.0
(Uomo del Futuro v2.0)
24: The Patriarchy
(Il Patriarcato)
25: Black Holes
(Buchi Neri)
26: Hidden Agenda
(Agenda Nascosta)
27: Don't Think about It
(Non ci Pensare)
28: You Can't Live a "Safe" Life
(Non Puoi Nivere Una Vita "Sicura")
29: Facial Expressions
(Espressioni Facciali)
30: We'll Talk Later
(Parliamo Più Tardi)
31: Be Sensible
(Essere Sensibile)
32: Take the Piss
(Prendere in Pisciare)
33: Queen Miriam
(Regina Miriam)
34: Creativity
(Creatività)

Contents

35: You're Not Going to Do Anything to Me Tonight
(Stanotte non mi Farai Niente)
36: Stop Being Sensible
(Smettila di essere Ragionevole)
37: Frequency
(Frequenza)
38: Ghost Riders on the Storm
(Cavalieri Fantasma nella Tempesta)
39: About Me
(Su di Me)
40: Dangerous
(Pericoloso)
41: Suffering
(Sofferenza)
42: If I Was Prime Minister (If You were Prime Minister)
Se Fossi il Primo Ministro (Se tu Fossi il Primo Ministro)
43: Take Nothing for Granted
(Non Dare Niente per Scontato)
44: Not Wearing a Mask is a Crime
(Non Indossare Una Maschera è un Crimine)
45: Attachment
(Allegato)
46: No Expectations
(Senza Aspettative)
47: (Into) The Night
(Nella Notte)
48: In the Category of "Friend"
(Nella Categoria "Amico")
49: I'm Writing the Script
(Sto Scrivendo la Sceneggiatura)
50: Access Granted
(Accesso Dato)

Am I Normal?

(Sono Normale?)

I don't want to get married.
I don't want to have children.
I don't want to become domesticated.
I don't want to stay at home.
Am I Normal?

I don't want to be boring.
I don't want to have a family.
I don't want to settle down.
Am I Normal?

I don't want to be an amoeba.
I don't want to be a single-celled organism.
I don't want to just eat & shit.
Am I Normal?

I don't want to just consume.
I don't want to just take.
I don't want to be alone.
Am I Normal?

I want to go out & have FUN.
I want to socialise & make friends.
I want to have a LIFE.
Am I Normal?

I want to discover myself.
I want to grow as a person.
I want to find internal happiness.
Am I Normal?

I want to be one with the Universe.
I want to be internally free.
I want to have no attachments.
Am I Normal?

"Because, I feel like I just don't fit in!"
Am I Normal?

"Yes, you are!"
"There is nothing wrong with you."
"What is normal anyway?"
"You just have to find your own tribe!"

(Based on a conversation with beautiful Suki)

"Well, all my friends are getting married
Yes, they're all growin' old
They're staying home on weekends
They're all doin' what they're told."

"Well sometimes I feel like I'm left behind
And sometimes I feel like I just left school
Wonder if I'll ever grow up
Maybe I'm the only fool"

Songwriter: Gregory J Macainsh
Performed by: Skyhooks

"The Don"
18.06.2021

He Has No Clue What's Going On
(Non ha Idea di cosa stia Succedendo)

He has no fucking idea.
He walks around with his head in the clouds.
Totally oblivious to what's happening around him.
He is just a bit player in a larger story.
But he's not aware of this.
Because...
...he has no clue what's going on.

He is being used.
He is not aware of this.
He is just a pawn.
He is just a puppet on a string.
Someone else is in control.
Someone else is pulling the strings.
Because...
...he has no clue what's going on.

Maybe it's better this way.
They say that *"ignorance is bliss"*!
Maybe it's better to be ignorant.
Rather than being aware & suffering.
He just seems to be happy in his own little world.
His own little bubble.
Because...
...he has no clue what's going on.

He doesn't stray very far.
He doesn't do very much.
He doesn't know many people.
He doesn't socialise much.
He's a very isolated individual.
Content to live in his bubble.
Because...
...he has no clue what's going on.

Maybe it's better that way!

"The Don"
18.06.2021

What Does it All Mean, Mr Jones?

(Cosa Significa tutto questo, Signor Jones?)

What is this all about?
What the fuck is happening here?
I have no fucking idea.
There is definitely something going on here
There is something happening here.
But....
...you don't know what it is, do you, Mr Jones?

I am lost in confusion.
I am confused in loss.
I don't know what the fuck it is.
But there is something definitely going on here.
Isn't there, Mr Jones?

I am intrigued & bewildered.
I am interested to see where this goes.
What the fuck is going on here?
Where is this all leading to...
...Mr Jones?

It is definitely an interesting ride.
It certainly isn't boring.
There are many twists & turns occurring.
I'm just sitting back & enjoying it.
Are you...?
...Mr Jones?

It's all a matter of interpretation.
It's all in the signals.
Just let it flow, bro.
Let it go where it needs to go, Mr Jones.

There is something definitely going on here.
But you don't know what it is, do you, Mr Jones.

It's certainly a lot of FUN though, Mr Jones!

"The Don"
19.06.2021

You're Killing Me with Music
(Mi stai Uccidendo con la Musica)

You're Killing me softly with your songs.
You're making LO♥E to me with your music.
I am captured by your embrace.
I am enraptured by your beauty.
I am a captured by your eyes.
I am a prisoner of this moment.
This delightful moment...
... *that I never want to end!*
I want it to last forever.
If *"forever"* is such a thing.

Don't let it stop.
Keep it going.
Killing me softly...
...with your words.
Killing me softly...
...with your songs
Killing me softly...
You're Killing Me with Music

Your intensity is insane.
Your energy is overwhelming.
Your power is immense.
Your aura is all encompassing.
I look into your eyes & I feel you.
I feel your passion.
I feel your desires.
I feel your suffering.
I feel your sadness.
I feel your happiness.
I feel you joy.
I feel you.

Still, you keep...
Killing me softly...
...with your words.
Killing me softly...
...with your songs
Killing me softly...
You're Killing Me with Music.

Your arms embrace me.
The hold me tight.
So close to you.
You hold me in your arms like a LO♥ER.

Still, you keep...
Killing me softly...
...with your words.
Killing me softly...
...with your songs
Killing me softly...
You're Killing Me with Music.

You're Killing Me with Music.
Don't stop.
Never stop.
Killing me softly...
...with your words.
Killing me softly...
...with your songs
Killing me softly...
You're Killing Me with Music.

"And it's a good way to die!"

"I heard he sang a good song, I heard he had a style
And so, I came to see him, to listen for a while
And there he was, this young boy, a stranger to my eyes."

"Strumming my pain with his fingers
Singing my life with his words
Killing me softly with his song
Killing me softly with his song
Telling my whole life with his words
Killing me softly with his song.

I felt all flushed with fever, embarrassed by the crowd
I felt he'd found my letters and read each one out loud
I prayed that he would finish, but he just kept right on.

Strumming my pain with his fingers
Singing my life with his words
Killing me softly with his song
Killing me softly with his song
Telling my whole life with his words.
Killing me softly.

Strumming my pain with his fingers
Singing my life with his words
Killing me softly with his song
Killing me softly with his song
Telling my whole life with his words
Killing me softly, with his words."

Songwriters: Norman Gimbel/Robin Spielberg/Charles Fox
Performed by: Roberta Flack

Inspired & dedicated to Miriam (my Soulmate in crime)

"The Don"
21.06.2021

Life is Not a Competition

(Non è una Competizione)

We're not in a competition.
We're not competitors on different sides.
Don't be competitive.
Don't be adversarial.
Life is not a competition.

We are not rivals.
I am not your enemy.
I don't want anything from you.
I don't need anything from you.
Life is not a competition.

Life is not a race.
There is no prize for coming first.
There is no prize for coming last.
The prize is the same for everyone.
No matter what position you come.
Remember...
Life is not a competition.

Let's not fight each other.
Let's not be enemies.
Let's not have hatred but be my companion.
Let's LO♥E each other instead.
Let's LO♥E & be friends...
...until the END.
...until the END.
...until the END.
Because...
Life is not a competition.

"You don't believe that, do you?"

"The Don"
21.06.2021

Die Before You Die

(Muori Prima di Morire)

Overcome your fears.
Overcome your suffering.
Overcome your angst.
Overcome your confusion.
Overcome your illusions.
Overcome your delusions.
Die before you die....
...and you will never DIE!

Conquer your fears
Conquer your suffering.
Conquer your angst.
Conquer your confusion.
Conquer your illusions.
Conquer your delusions.
Die before you die....
...and you will never DIE!

We live in fear.
Our whole life is filled with fear.
It is there as soon as we realise that we are not immortal.
That we will die.
That we are born to die.
We will not live forever.
We are not immortal.
Die before you die....
...and you will never DIE!

It's all about the fear of Death.
Face the fear of Death.
Look Death in the eyes.
Grab Death by the throat.
Strangle the Life out of Death.
Conquer the fear of Death.
Die before you die....
...and you will never DIE!

Die before you die & the is no DEATH.

He who dies BEFORE he dies will NEVER die!

Overcome your fear of Death & you will become IMMORTAL!
Nothing can hurt you...
...not even Death.

"The Don"
22.06.2021

Your Protector

(Il tuo Protettore)

I'll keep you safe.
I will look after you.
I will be there for you.
I will never let you down.
I will shelter you, if you need shelter.
I will LO♥E you, if you need LO♥E.
I will be your friend, when you need a friend.
I will listen, when you need to be heard.
I will let you cry, if you need to cry.
I will make LO♥E with you, if you want to make LO♥E.
Because...
...I am your protector.

I promise I won't let you down.
I know I have let you down before.
But I suffered for it.
As you have told me that you also suffered.
We both suffered.
I regret it.
It was regrettable.
But I have learnt.
I have grown.
I am a better person.
I want to be a better friend.
I want to be a better Human Being.
That's why I can now say...
...I am your protector.

I will not let you down this time.
But it's not just about you.
It's about everyone who is my friend.
To all of you...
...I will not you down.
I will always be there for you.
If you need me.
When you need me.
But for you...
...I will always be there for you.
I will be your protector.

But to you...
...you who are so special to me.
...you who are so important to me.
...you who are my *"Soulmate"*.
I will NEVER let you down.
I will always be with you.
You are no longer alone.
I will be there either physically...
...or
... emotionally.
I will always support you.
I will always have your back.
You can rest on me.
You can lean on me.
You can depend on me.
...I will always be there for you.
I am your protector.

"You can rely on me."
"Do you trust me?"

"The Don"
22.06.2021

The Establishment

(L'istituzione)

It is The System.
It is a structure.
It is an organisation.
It controls everyone.
It controls everything.
It makes all the rules.
It makes all the laws.
It decides what is right & what it is wrong.
It decides who is guilty & who is not.
It decides who is punished.
It decides what punishment it is.
It has the power of Life & Death.
It decides who lives & who dies.
It is governed by men.
It is Patriarchal.
It is a Patriarchy.
Fuck the Establishment.
Let's rebel against the Establishment.
Let's bring down the Establishment.
Let's destroy the Establishment.
Let's have a REVOLUTION!

"Are you with me?"
"YES!!!"
"But..."
"... can I just finish off my breakfast first?'
"It's the most important meal of the day..."
"...or so they say."

"The Don"
23.06.2021

Power Corrupts

(Corruzioni di Potere)

What is "Power"?
Power is control over others.
It can be control over just one person...
...or it can be control over many people.
It means making decisions for them.
Instead of allowing people to make decisions for themselves.
Denying them self-expression.
Denying them individuality.
Denying them freedom.
Subjugating them to...
...your will.
...your desires.
...your wants.
...your needs.
...your personal interests.
...your selfish appetites.
Power is about *"Ego"*.
Power feeds the *"Ego"*.
This, is why...
... power corrupts.

An individual can't help it.
Power goes straight to one's head.
Power inflates one's Ego.
Power cannot be controlled.
Power cannot be contained.
Power is contagious.
Power is infectious.
Power is a disease.
Power is a mental disease.
Power corrupts the Mind!

Power distorts the individual's self-worth.
They start to believe that they are more important than everyone else.
That the world cannot survive without them.
That they know better than everyone else.
That their opinion is more important than everyone else's.
This is delusional.
This leads one to become a psychopath.
Do not give an individual or a small group of people power.
Because they won't be able to handle it.
No matter what they say.
The human psyche cannot cope with *power*.
It is not designed for it.
This is why *power corrupts.*

There is no other way.
There are no alternatives.
Power corrupts.

So be careful to whom you give *the Power.*
Because...
...*power corrupts.*

"The Don"
23.06.2021

The Ego

(L'ego)

The Ego wants to dominate.
The Ego wants to control.
The Ego has no fear.
The Ego is delusional.

Do not inflate *the Ego*.
Do not let it grow out of proportion.
Do not feed *the Ego*.
Do not let *the Ego* grow.

Keep *the Ego* in check.
Keep *the Ego* under control.
Keep *the Ego* securely restrained.
Keep *the Ego* constrained.

The Ego will fight.
The Ego will want to dominate.
The Ego will try to escape.
The Ego will not rest.
The Ego will struggle to be free.
The Ego will cajole you.
The Ego will flatter you.
The Ego will delude you.
The Ego will plead with you.
The Ego will cry for mercy.
The Ego will beg you for forgiveness.
The Ego will keep knocking at your door.
The Ego will be relentless.
The Ego will never stop...
...until you are DEAD!

"Are you up for the fight?"
"I don't think so!"

"The Don"
23.06.2021

No One Else Can See You Like I See You
(Nessun Altro Può Vederti Come ti Vedo Io)

No one else can feel you like I feel you.
No one else can hear you like I hear you.
No one else can understand you like I understand you.
No one else can know you like I know you.
No one else can empathise with you like I empathise with you.
No one else can LO♥E you like LO♥E you.
Because...
...no one else can see you like I see you.

It's our special bond.
It's our special connection.
It's our special friendship.
It's our special LO♥E.
It's our special something.
It's our special cosmic force.
It's our special cosmic energy.
Because...
...no one else can see you like I see you.

I can't explain it.
I can't understand it.
I can't comprehend it.
I can't fathom it.
I can't figure it out.
I can't rationalise it.
I can't intellectualise it
I can only say that...
...no one else can see you like I see you.

That's it.
There's nothing more to say.
That's all there is to it.
No one else can see you like I see you.

"The Don"
23.06.2021

I Am Weak

(Io Sono Debole)

I give in too easily.
I let my emotions control me.
I let my emotions take over.
I let my emotions make decisions for me.
I am weak.

I have no will power.
I have no internal fortitude.
I have no internal strength.
I have no staying power.
I am weak.

I'm just too soft.
Call me *"Jelly Belly"*.
I'm as weak as piss *(although piss can be quite strong if it's concentrated)*.
I'm pathetic.
I'm a loser.
I am weak.

I need to be strong.
I need to resist temptation.
I need to hold my resolve.
I need to control my emotions.
Because…
…I am weak.

I admit it.
It's true.
I can't deny it.
I have to face reality.
I have to face myself.
I have to look into the mirror & say...
...I am weak.

Accept your weakness.
Face your weakness.
Challenge your weakness.
Control your weakness.
Defeat your weakness.
Because...
...I am weak.

"I am a weakling!"
"But when I grow up, I want to be strong!"

"The Don"
24.06.2021

I Am a Looney

(Io Sono un Pazzo)

I am a looney & I am proud.
I don't want to be normal.
I don't want to be like everyone else.
I don't want to be sane.
I don't want to be just one of the crowd.
I don't want to follow the crowd.
I don't want to be a sheep.
I am don't want to be beige.
I don't want to be grey.
I want to be different.
I am different.
I am an individual.
I am crazy.
I am insane.
I am a looney.

Call me crazy.
Call me insane.
Call me eccentric.
Call me weird.
Call me whatever you like.
I don't care.
Because...
...I am a looney.

I am a looney & I am proud.
I am a looney & I'll shout it out loud.
I am a looney & I don't care what you think.
I am a looney & I don't care even if you think I stink.
Because I know...
...I am a looney.

I am a looney & I stand proud!

"The Don"
24.06.2021

I'm Bad

(Io Sono Cattivo)

I try to be good...
...but I'm a failure.
I can't help it.
I sin.
I'm a sinner.
I'm a sinner man.
What can I do?
I'm bad.

There's nothing I can do about it.
I try to be good...
...but I'm a failure.
I can't help it.
I'm the Devil's child.
I'm a Heathen man.
But what can I do about it?
I'm bad.

I don't go to church.
I don't pray to God.
Fuck, I don't even believe in God.
Man, I'm REALLY bad.
I try to be good...
...but I'm a failure.
I can't help it.
I'm just bad.

"I think I was born bad!"

"Because I'm bad, I'm bad come on (Really really bad)
You know I'm bad, I'm bad you know it (Really really bad)
You know I'm bad, I'm bad come on, you know (Really really bad)
And the whole world has to answer right now
Just to tell you once again
Who's bad?"

Performed by: Michael Jackson
Songwriters: Dallas Austin/Michael Joe Jackson/Rene Moore/Bruce F Swedien

"The Don"
24.06.2021

Hidden in the Darkness

(Nascosto nell'Oscurità)

Lurking in the shadows.
Staying out of sight.
Never in the daylight.
Only comes out at night.
He is the *"Darkness"*.
He is the man without a face.
He has no identity.
He has no home.
He has no place
He is...
...hidden in the Darkness.

The darkness is his friend.
The shadows are his home.
He does not belong here.
He belongs in another place.
He is not of this reality.
This is not his home.
He is an outsider here.
That is why...
...he is hidden in the Darkness.

He comes from another dimension.
He comes from another Universe.
He comes from another time & space.
He comes from the past & the future.
He comes from *"Dark Matter"*.
He comes from the *"Darkness"*.
He is hidden in the *"Darkness"*.
Because...
...he is "Darkness" itself!

"The Don"
24.06.2021

We Are All the Same

(Siamo Tutti Uguali)

Remove our exterior covering.
Throw away all the external layers.
Take off all your clothes.
Expose yourself with nothing on.
Stand naked for everyone to see.
There in your *"Birthday suit"*.
The way you were born.
The way we were all born...
...naked.
We are all the same.

This is what we forget.
This is what our clothes hide.
This what our coverings protect.
This is who we really are.
This is what we cannot hide.
This is what we must see.
This is what we have to admit.
This is what we have to confront.
This is what we cannot run away from.
This how we were born.
We were born naked.
And when we stand naked...
...we see that...
...we are all the same.

We are all HUMANS!
All made of the same stuff...
... flesh & blood, skin & bones.
Nothing separates us...
...except our thoughts.
...except our ideas.
...except our values.
...except our culture.
...except our MINDS.
We are all the same.

Don't let our minds separate us.
Don't let our minds divide us.
Because when we stand naked...
...we see that...
...we are all the same.

Yes, we are all the same.
And we are all BEAUTIFUL.
We are all Human.
We are all the same.

We are all the same!
If we can remember that...
...we are all the same.
Then this world would be a far better place

We are all the same!

We are all the same!

We are all the same!

We are all the same!

" Except me, of course!"
"I'm only joking!"
"God, people can't take a joke anymore!"
"Everyone's lost their sense of humour!"

"The Don"
25.06.2021

Our Mind

(La Nostra Mente)

Our Mind doesn't exist!
Not physically, anyway.
And then maybe, not even psychologically either.
Our mind is a Human construct.
It is an illusion.
It is a delusion.

Our Mind creates problems when there are no problems.
Our Mind creates fantasies.
Our Mind creates justifications.
Our Mind creates excuses.
Our Mind creates differences between us.
Our Mind divides us.
Our Mind destroys us!

Let us not be ruled by *our Mind*.
Let us not be controlled by *our Mind*.
Let us not be dictated by *our Mind*.
Let us not be governed by *our Mind*.
Let us not be captured by *our Mind*.
Let us not be held captive by *our Mind*.
Let us not be held prisoner by *our Mind*.

Our Mind is our enemy.
It works against us.
It plans against us.
It plots again us.
It strategises against us.
It lies to us.
It manipulates us.
It uses us.
It abuses us.
And ultimately...
...it destroys us!
Our Mind is a destroyer!

Let us rebel against *our Mind.*
Let us break free from *our Mind.*
Let us live without *our Mind.*
Let us be *"Mind-less".*

Let us shout...
"I have no mind!"
"I am Mind-less"!"
"And I LO♥E it!"

"The Don"
25.06.2021

Jealousy

(Gelosia)

Jealousy is a curse.
Jealousy is a disease.
Jealousy is a demon.
Jealousy is insidious.
Jealousy is a plague.
Jealousy is a virus.
Jealousy is a contagion.
Jealousy is contagious.
Jealousy is a contamination.
Jealousy is an infection.
Jealousy is diabolical.
Jealousy is destructive.
Jealousy is debilitating.
Jealousy is destructive.
Jealousy is nihilistic.
Jealousy is inebriating.
Jealousy is darkness.
Jealousy is destructive.
Jealousy is immobilising.
Jealousy is hatred.
Jealousy is deadly.
Jealousy is DEATH

Destroy jealousy.
Destroy jealousy before it destroys you!

"The Don"
25.06.2021

La Luna

(The Moon)

"La Luna" watches over me.
It speaks to me.
It says, *"Don't worry, everything will be alright."*
"I will look after you."
"I will protect you."
"I will make sure that you are fine."
"I will make sure everything works out."

I listen to *"La Luna"*.
I trust it.
I look up at it.
I see it looking down upon me.
And I smile.
Because I am happy.

I know it is shining its light upon me.
I know it can see me.
I know it understands me.
I know we share a bond.
A profound connection.
We communicate to each other.
We speak the same language.
The language of LO♥E.

"La Luna" is intimate.
"La Luna" is embracing.
"La Luna" is encompassing.
"La Luna" is nurturing.
"La Luna" is caring.
"La Luna" is LO♥ING.

I trust *"La Luna"*.
Maybe you should too.
"La Luna" won't let you down.

"The Don"
25.06.2021

ACCESS DENIED

(Accesso Negato)

ACCESS DENIED.
Until permission is granted.
ACCESS DENIED.
Until permission is given.
ACCESS DENIED.
Insufficient clearance.
ACCESS DENIED.
Insufficiently accredited.
ACCESS DENIED.
Inadequate level.
ACCESS DENIED.
Inappropriate grade.
ACCESS DENIED.
Not your pay grade.
ACCESS DENIED.
Security risk.
ACCESS DENIED.
Suspicious character.
ACCESS DENIED.
More training required.
ACCESS DENIED.
Intellectually challenged.
ACCESS DENIED.
Visually impaired.
ACCESS DENIED.
Vertically challenged.
ACCESS DENIED.
Mentally deficient.
ACCESS DENIED.
Hair too short.
ACCESS DENIED.
Sexually inadequate.
ACCESS DENIED.
Does not satisfy "shlong" length requirements.
ACCESS DENIED.
Personality deficit.

Can I give you a cuddle?
ACCESS DENIED.
Can I give you a hug?
ACCESS DENIED.
Can I touch you knee?
ACCESS DENIED.
Can I sit next to you?
ACCESS DENIED.
Can I touch your feet?
ACCESS DENIED.
Can I touch you down there?
ACCESS DENIED.
Can I touch you anywhere?
ACCESS DENIED.
Try later.
ACCESS DENIED.
System maintenance.
ACCESS DENIED.
Incorrect code.
ACCESS DENIED.
Intruder alert.
ACCESS DENIED.
Alien.
ACCESS DENIED.
Non-Human!
ACCESS DENIED.
Non-Human!
ACCESS DENIED.
Non-Human!
ACCESS DENIED.
ACCESS DENIED.
ACCESS DENIED.
ACCESS DENIED.
ACCESS DENIED.
ACCESS DENIED.
ACCESS DENIED.
ACCESS DENIED.

(Based on a conversation had with my best friend with "some benefits", Miriam)

"The Don"
28.06.2021

Look on the Bright Side of Death
(Guarda il Lato Positivo della Morte)

No more going to work *(a permanent retirement)*.
No more doing a job that you hate.
No more of that, 9 to 5 shit.
No more worrying about what to cook for dinner.
No more worries about what to wear.
No more worries FOREVER!
No more paying rent.
No more mortgage.
No more bills, period.
No more speeding fines.
No more paying taxes.
No more politicians *(& their bullshit)*.
No more health issues.
No more sorrow.
No more sadness.
No more pain.
No more fears.
No more getting rejected.
No more struggling.
No more self-image issues *(not me, of course)*.
No more sexual frustrations.
No more unrequited LO❤E.
No more getting old.
No more fear of DEATH.

There is so much more to Death than one realises.
So...
...look on the bright side of DEATH!

"The Don"
27.06.2021

How Does One Grow Old?
(Come Si Invecchia?)

Does one accept it?
Does one fight it?
Does one challenge it?
Does one deny it?
Does one resist it?
Does one neutralise it?
Does one succumb to it?
Does one not accept it?
Does one bring it on?
Does one forget about it?
Does one meditate about it?
Does one destroy it?
Does one celebrate it?
Does one write poems about it?
Does one figure it out?
How does one get old?

"Resistance is futile"

"I'm getting old disgracefully?"
"And it's working!"

"The Don"
27.06.2021

Future Man v2.0

(Uomo del Futuro v2.0)

He has no past.
He has no present.
He doesn't exist yet.
He is not here yet.
He is of the FUTURE.
He is Future Man v2.0

He has no fears.
He has no doubts.
He has no inhibitions.
He has no hatred.
He is Future Man v2.0

He is completely new.
He is next year's model.
He is new & improved.
He is the BEST there's ever been.
He is everything you've EVER wanted.
He is Future Man v2.0

He is empathetic.
He is kind.
He is caring.
He is compassionate.
He is LO♥ING.
He is Future Man v2.0

He is made for *adventure*.
He is made for *having FUN*.
He is made for *DANCING*.
He is made for *PARTYING*.
He is made for *ROCK & ROLL*.
He is Future Man v2.0

He is a *"secret agent man"*.
He is a *"Phantom Agent"*.
He is an *"Agent of Change"*.
He is an *"Agent Provocateur"*
He is an *"Agent of Chaos"*.
He is Future Man v2.0

He will NEVER let you down.
He will ALWAYS be there for you.
He will ALWAYS be your friend.
He will ALWAYS support you.
He will only use his cock if you want him to.
He is Future Man v2.0

"The Don"
29.06.2021

The Patriarchy

(Il Patriarcato)

Men rule.
Men have ALWAYS ruled.
Men have ALWAYS dominated.
Men have ALWAYS been dominant.
Men have ALWAYS controlled.
Men are The Patriarchy.

Patriarchy is endemic.
Patriarchy is pandemic.
Patriarchy is epidemic.
Patriarchy is systemic.
Men are The Patriarchy.

Patriarchy is a disease.
Patriarchy is a scourge.
Patriarchy is a system.
Patriarchy is a way of thinking.
Men are The Patriarchy.

Patriarchy must be stopped.
Patriarchy must be destroyed.
Patriarchy is over.
Patriarchy is finished.
Men are The Patriarchy.

Patriarchy is DEAD!

RIT (Rest in Torment) Patriarchy!

"The Don"
29.06.2021

Black Holes

(Buchi Neri)

"Black Holes do exist!"
"They're not just in Space."
"They are right here too."
"There are many here among us right now!"
"You might know one."
"You might be one (although you won't admit it)!"

Some people have no *personality*.
Some people have no *humour*.
Some people have no FUN.
Some people have no *friends*.
Some people have no LIFE.
Some people are *"Black Holes"*.

They consume energy from those around them.
They suck the *"Life Force"* of others.
They leave you empty.
They leave you exhausted.
They have sucked you dry.
They have taken your *VITALITY*.
They are *"Black Holes"*.

They have nothing to give.
They have nothing to offer.
They are completely empty.
They are devoid of any energy of their own.
They have no vitality.
They have no *"Life Force"*.
They are leaches sucking you dry.
They are vampires.
They have no LIFE.
They are DEAD.
They are *"Black Holes"*.

"Stay away from such people."
"Otherwise, you will become one of the "walking DEAD!"

"The Don"
30.06.2021

Hidden Agenda

(Agenda Nascosta)

Everyone's got one.
What's hidden beneath your facade?
What is locked up in your closet *(for no one to see)*?
What are you hiding under that pretty, pretty face?
What is your "Hidden Agenda"?

Are you looking for friends?
Are you searching for fame & fortune?
Are you seeking the *"Fountain of Youth"*?
Are you looking for sex?
Are you looking for passion?
Are you looking for desire?
Are you looking for LO❤E?
What is your "Hidden Agenda"?

Do you want power?
Do you want money?
Do you want control?
Do you want domination?
Do you want eternal youth?
Do you want sex?
Do you want to be liked?
Do you want to be LO❤ED?
What is your "Hidden Agenda"?

"I just want to be a "Superstar" (but everybody knows that)!"
"Oh yeah, I already am!"
"Is that bad?"
"Hahahahaha!"

"The Don"
30.06.2021

Don't Think about It

(Non ci Pensare)

Don't waste your time thinking.
Just take it as it comes.
Don't try to outwit the Universe.
Don't try to outsmart it.
Don't try to outthink it.
You won't win.
Don't think!
Just...
...don't think about it.

You have better things to do with your time.
You have loftier ambitions.
You have FUN to be enjoyed.
You have to PARTY down.
You have to *"ROCK ON"*.
You have a LIFE to live.
Don't think about it.

Let things happen.
Let things flow.
Let things go.
Let things evolve independently of you.
Let things develop of their own accord.
Let things grow as they should.
Let things flourish as they will.
Don't think about it.

"Oops, I just thought about it!"
"Goddam!"

"I have to STOP thinking about it!"

(Based on a conversation, inspired & dedicated to my friend, Ceren)

"The Don"
01.07.2021

You Can't Live a "Safe" Life

(Non Puoi Nivere Una Vita "Sicura")

You can't live without taking risks.
You can't live without taking chances.
You can't live without living on the edge.
You can't live without coming out of your hole.
You can't live life without getting out there.
You can't live life without playing the game.
You can't live life without living it.
You can't live a "safe" life.

Life is full of risks.
Life is full of challenges.
Life is full of setbacks.
Life is full of roundabouts.
Life is full of curves.
Life is full of sadness.
Life is full of rejection.
Life is full of loneliness.
Life is full of adventures.
You can't live a "safe" life.

So don't play it safe.
Don't stay in your *"comfort zone"*.
Break out.
Take a leap...
...into the unknown.
...into the river.
...into chaos.
...into unpredictability.
...into the world.
...into adventure.
... into LO♥E.
Don't live a *"safe"* life.
You can't live a "safe" life.

"The Don"
02.07.2021

Facial Expressions

(Espressioni Facciali)

She has so many expressions.
Her face twists & turns.
It contorts into all these different shapes.
She twists her mouth.
She raises her eyebrows.
She screws her mouth.
She purses her lips.
She furrows her brow.
Her mouth suggests of things to come.
She begins to grin.
She releases a smile.
She starts to laugh.
Just a giggle at first.
Then it gets bigger.
She sways her head backwards.
She is now in full flight.
It is wholehearted *"belly laugh"*.
It grows into a crescendo.
She is really enjoying it.
Tears swell up in her eyes.
They start to run down her cheeks.
She is happy.
She has no worries in the world.
She has no cares.
She is *"living in the moment"*.
She is now HAPPY!

"It's so good to see her like this."
"In a state of pure Bliss!"
"Without a worry in the world!"

(Inspired & dedicated to Miriam)

"The Don"
02.07.2021

We'll Talk Later

(Parliamo Più Tardi)

Later...
...how much later?
...an hour?
...two hours?
...three hours?
...a day?
...a couple of days?
...a week?
...a couple of weeks?
...a month?
How much later?

We'll talk later...
...how much later?

This is such a non-specific term.
It is so vague as to be almost nonsensical.
It means nothing.
It's an empty statement.
It has no beginning.
It has no end.

We'll talk later...
...how much later?

Give me an idea.
Give me a clue.
Give me some sort of timeframe to work with.
Don't leave it open-ended.
Don't be so loose.
It just does my head in.

We'll talk later...
...how much later?

"I think it means, don't ring me, I'll ring you!"
"NEVER!"

"I'm still waiting!"
"Because..."Later" NEVER comes!"

"The Don"
03.07.2021

Be Sensible

(Essere Sensibile)

Clean up your act.
Get you act together.
Stop drinking.
Stay sober.
Play the game.
Play your *"A"* grade game.
Stay focused.
Be where you wanna be.
Stay strong.
Sort yourself out.
Sort out your shit.
Sort your shit out.
Get it together.
Get back on track.
This is not where you wanna be.
FUCK this shit.
Become sensible.
BE sensible!

"Relax!"
"You overthink too much!"
"You're driving yourself crazy!"

"The Don"
03.07.2021

Take the Piss

(Prendere in Pisciare)

Nothing is *serious*.
Nothing is *"Real"*.
Nothing is *"Forever"*.
Nothing is *infinite*.
So.....take the piss out EVERYTHING.

There is no *"Happy ending"*.
There is no *"pot of gold.*
There is no *"Everlasting LO♥E"*.
There is no *"Tomorrow!"*
So.....take the piss out EVERYTHING.

Take the piss out of...
...*society*.
Take the piss out of...
...*the education system*.
Take the piss out of...
... *politicians*.
Take the piss out of...
... *politics*.
Take the piss out of...
...*the government*.
Take the piss out of...
...*the lawmakers*.
Take the piss out of...
... *religion*.
Take the piss out of...
...*LIFE*
Take the piss out of...
...*DEATH*.
Take the piss out of...
...*of me*.
Take the piss out of...
... *YOURSELF!*

Just......take the piss out of EVERYTHING!

"That's the ONLY way to survive in this crazy world that we live in!"

"The Don"
03.07.2021

Queen Miriam

(Regina Miriam)

She just has to put out her hand.
And her request is met.
With a quick flick of the wrist
And your request is denied.
"Can I put something on, me Lady?"
Her reply is as quick as it is precise.
"No!"
She says without raising her head.
She doesn't have to, because...
...she is "Queen Miriam".

She gestures with her fingers.
Her small, yet delicate hand.
No words are uttered from her mouth
Yet I know exactly what she requires.
I have to.
It's what I do.
I am there to serve...
..."Queen Miriam"

"Another beer"!
I quickly get up & make my way to the fridge.
I walk tall, straightish & proud.
I try to deport myself well.
I try to maintain my poise.
I am after all from Italian pedigree.
I have a reputation to keep.
Not only for myself & my country.
But also, for...
..."Queen Miriam".

Her request is met.
She is happy.
I am happy that she is happy.
That's all I want to do.
Is to make her happy.
I am not successful all the time.
But I do succeed sometimes.
Which is, I guess all that one can ask for.
From...
..."Queen Miriam".

"She also lives in "The Lodge", (as she should & deserves)!

(Inspired & dedicated to Miriam)

"The Don"
04.07.2020

Creativity

(Creatività)

Creativity will *save you.*
Creativity will *set you free.*
Creativity will *open your mind.*
Creativity will *open your Future.*
Creativity will *give you, LIFE.*
Creativity will *give you HOPE.*
Creativity will *ignite your PASSION.*
Creativity will *set you on FIRE.*
Creativity will *fuel your DESIRE.*
Creativity will *be your friend.*
Creativity will *be there until the END.*
Creativity will *NOT let you down.*
Creativity will *always be around.*
Creativity will *stop your sadness.*
Creativity will *put an end to ALL your doubts.*
Creativity will *give you faith in yourself.*
Creativity will *take you to new places.*
Creativity will *be an adventure.*
Creativity will *be your saviour.*

Creativity will *save you.*
Creativity will *set you free.*
Creativity will *open your mind.*
Creativity will *open your Future.*

"Creativity will even save you from dementia!"

"The Don"
06.07.2021

You're Not Going to Do Anything to Me Tonight
(Stanotte non mi Farai Niente)

You're not going to touch me tonight.
You're not going to hold me tonight.
You're not going to hug me tonight.
You're not going to cuddle me tonight.
You're not going to kiss me tonight.
You're not going to sleep with me tonight.
You're not going to make LO♥E to me tonight.
You're not going to do anything to me tonight.

You're just going to look at me tonight.
You're just going to sing for me tonight.
You're just going to dance for me tonight.
You're just going to laugh with me tonight.
You're just going to play guitar for me tonight.
You're just going to have FUN with me tonight.
You're just going to make me HAPPY tonight.
But...
...you're not going to sleep me tonight.
...you're not going to make LO♥E to me tonight.
...you're not going to do anything to me tonight.

You're not going to kiss me tonight.
You're not going to sleep me tonight.
You're not going to make LO♥E to me tonight.
You're not going to do anything to me tonight.

"The Don"
06.07.2021

Stop Being Sensible

(Smettila di essere Ragionevole)

Stop being a *follower*.
Stop being a *slave*.
Stop being *controlled*.
Stop being *told what to do*.
Stop being a *puppet on a string*.
Stop being a *prisoner*.
Stop being sensible.

Stop being a part of *The System*.
Stop being a part of *The Establishment*.
Stop being a part of *The Patriarchy*.
Stop being a part of *"The Machine"*.
Stop being a part of *The Autocracy*.
Stop being a part of *"The Conservative Non-Thinkers"*.
Stop being sensible.

Be whoever you want to be.
Do whatever you want to do.
Think whatever you want to think.
LO♥E whomever you want to LO♥E.
Be whomever you want to BE.
DON'T listen to anyone else.
Be Yourself!
Stop being sensible.

Be *INSANE*, if you want to be.
Be *CRAZY*, if you want to be.
Be *MAD*, if you want to be.
Be a *LOONEY*, it you want to be.
Be an *ANARCHIST*, if you want to be.
Be an A*NTICHRIST*, if you want to be.
Be a *REBEL*, if you want to be.
Be a *REVOLUTIONARY*, if you want to be.
Be an *ANTI-ESTABLISHMENTARIANIST*, if you want to.
But...
...stop being sensible.

"Being "SENSIBLE" doesn't work!"
"It's NOT you!"

So...
...stop being sensible.

"The Don"
06.07.2021

Frequency

(Frequenza)

It's all in the vibrations.
It's all in the energy.
It's all in the synchronicity.
It's all in the connection.
It's all on the *FREQUENCY*.

It's all about being in tune.
It's all about being in phase.
It's all about transmission.
It's all about reception.
It's all about wavelength.
It's all on the *FREQUENCY*.

There's nothing you can do about it.
There's nothing you can say about it.
There is nothing you can think about it.
There is nothing you can plan about it.
There is nothing you can control about it.
It's all on the *FREQUENCY*.

It's all about modulation.
It's all about attenuation.
It's all about calibration.
It's all about wave energy.
It's all about Hertz (Hz).
It's all on the *FREQUENCY*.

It's all in the vibrations.
It's all in the energy.
It's all in the synchronicity.
It's all in the connection.
It's all on the *FREQUENCY*.

"The Don"
06.07.2021

Ghost Riders on the Storm
(Cavalieri Fantasma nella Tempesta)

They come from a far off land.
Nobody really knows from where.
They come to cleanse the Earth.
They come to cleanse the land.
Ghost Riders on the Storm.

With a burst of thunder & flashing strikes of lightening.
They descend out of the Heavens.
In a blaze of doom & gloom.
They appear out of nowhere.
Ghost Riders on the Storm.

Their work is swift.
Their work is quick.
They ride majestically across the skies.
On their white horses made from clouds.
Ghost Riders on the Storm.

They cross the sky from left to right.
And then back again.
They never stop until their work is done.
On the fourth pass, which is their last.
Their work is done.
Ghost Riders on the Storm.

The disappear just as they came.
They ascend back in the Heavens from whence they came.
Their mission accomplished.
Their work done.
Ghost Riders on the Storm.

They came to clean the land of *hatred.*
They came to clean the land of *injustices.*
They came to clean the land of *inequalities.*
They came to clean the land of *discrimination.*
Ghost Riders on the Storm.

"The Don"
06.07.2021

About Me

(Su di Me)

I thought that I tell you something *"About Me"*, myself.
So that you can get to know me better.
Not that you don't know me already.
To start off with, I have to tell you straight off...
...that I am the *BEST!*
In fact, there's nobody else like me!
I am *UNIQUE!*
But I guess you guys already knew that.
It's quite obvious isn't it.
I'm stating the bleeding obvious, ain't I?
That's because there's only ONE of me in the whole Cosmos.
I'm *IRREPLACEABLE!*
Once I'm gone, there'll *NEVER* be another me.
And you're probably thinking, *"good fucking riddance!"*

But I'm not saying anything new.
You guys already know this.
Because you are also *UNIQUE*.
Just like me.
Well, not exactly like me.
I'm way better, of course.
That goes without saying.

Now, what was I saying?
I lost my train of thought for a moment.
Oh yes, I was going to tell you something about myself.
Ok, first of all I think you should all know that I *"Self-Medicate"*.
I don't trust doctors, so I diagnose myself.
I make a prognosis & then prescribe drugs.

I LO♥E taking drugs.
The more the better.
I have NEVER stuffed from any side- effects.
And I have been taking drugs over a very long period.
In fact, my whole life.
And as you can plainly see for yourself.
I am COMPLETELY fine.
I am COMPLETELY healthy.
I am COMPLETELY normal.

In fact, I am quite an incredible example of the male human species.
And I believe, it's all down to my drug taking.
So, I highly recommend & encourage all of you to take drugs…
…if you're not doing so already.
Take as many as you can.
That's my advice.

Another thing that I think you should know about me.
Which I will tell you now.
Is…
…I also *"Self-Analyse"* myself.
YEP!
I've never gone to see a *"Shrink"*.
I haven't had too.
Not that I think they're any good.
I think they're just a waste of money.

Anyway, you can clearly see for yourselves, that I am a COMPLETELY sane individual.
Totally in control of his mental faculties.
Intellectually sharp.
Emotionally secure.
A perfect example of a human being balanced, centred & equilibrated.
In touch with his Chi!

So, I implore everyone to do the same thing.
"Self-analyse" yourself.
You reap the benefits immediately.
You can take my word on that.

"Anyway, I hope that this knowledge "About Me" will be of some use to you."
"It's been the "bed-rock" of my life."
"And look at me now."
"An AWESOME human being."
"If I so myself!"

"The Don"
07.07.2021

Dangerous

(Pericoloso)

I am dangerous.
I am crazy.
I am mad.
I am insane.
I am ridiculous.
I am zany.
I am curious.
I am extreme.
I am DANGEROUS.

I will burn you.
I will turn you.
I will scare you
I will tear you.
I will excite you.
I will incite you.
I will hurt you.
I will like you.
I will LO♥E you.
I am DANGEROUS.

Stay away from me.
Walk away from me.
Run away from me.
Crawl away from me.
Hide away from me.
Slink away from me.
Slither away from me.
Fade away from me.
Because...
...I am DANGEROUS.

"Just saying!"

"The Don"
09.07.2021

Suffering

(Sofferenza)

Suffering, what a pain in the arse it is.
Suffering it's so debilitating.
Suffering is so unnecessary.
Suffering is so "Real".
Suffering, I HATE it.
Suffering is debilitating.
Suffering is crippling.
Suffering is suffocating.
Suffering is excruciating.
Suffering is disheartening.
Suffering is mind-numbing.
Suffering is a disease.
Suffering is a killer.
Suffering is deadly.
Suffering is DEATH!

Suffering is useless.
Suffering is unnecessary.
Suffering is self-induced.
Suffering is illusory.
Suffering is all in your head.
Suffering is all in your mind.
Suffering is optional.
Suffering is a choice.
Suffering is YOUR choice.

Suffering is all in your head.
Suffering is all in your mind.

In your head.
In your head.
In your head.
In your head!

"The Don"
09.07.2021

If I Was Prime Minister
(If You were Prime Minister)

Se Fossi il Primo Ministro (Se tu Fossi il Primo Ministro)

What would you do?
What would I do?
I would...
...not lie.
...have integrity.
...have principles
...do what I say.
...not make promises I could not keep.
...be held accountable for my actions.
...be held accountable for my decisions.
...consult.
...be a conduit for the voice of the people.
...let people decide.
...ask the people.
...end discrimination.
...end exploitation.
...introduce equity & equality in everything.
...make sure that basic human rights are met.
...make things right.
...save the planet
...change the world.
...make society a better place!
...make the world a BETTER place!
That's what I would do!

"That's just to start off with!"
"What would you do if you were Prime Minister?"

"The Don"
09.07.2021

Take Nothing for Granted
(Non Dare Niente per Scontato)

Assume nothing.
Expect nothing.
Nothing is certain.
Nothing is fixed.
Everything is fluidic.
Everything is unpredictable.
Everything is CHAOS.
Take nothing for granted.

Things NEVER happen as you expect them to.
Things NEVER happen as you want them to.
Things NEVER work out like you planned them to.
Things NEVER follow a straight line.
Things NEVER follow a straight path.
Things are NEVER predicable.
Things are NEVER foreseeable.
Things are NEVER foreseen.
Things are NEVER forewarned.
Take nothing for granted.

Expect the unexpected.
Expect the unforeseen.
Expect the uncertainty.
Expect the randomness.
Expect the CHAOS.
Expect the FAILURE.
Expect the LOSS
Expect the REJECTION.
Expect the DEATH.
Take nothing for granted.

"The Don"
09.07.2021

Not Wearing a Mask is a Crime
(Non Indossare Una Maschera è un Crimine)

Not such a long time ago...
... wearing a mask was a crime!
What's happened?
What's turned things upside down?
That people are being…
…arrested.
…punished.
…penalised.
…fined.
…criminalised.
…ostracised.
…humiliated.
…shamed.
…victimised.
…for NOT wearing a mask!

"You are BAD person!"
"You are a criminal!"
"You will be punished!"
"You will be fined!"
"You will be prosecuted!"
"You might go to prison!"
…for NOT wearing a mask!

"The Don"
09.07.2021

Attachment

(Allegato)

Attachment is a curse.
Attachment is a disease.
Attachment is a plague.
Attachment is debilitating.
Attachment is destructive.
Attachment is consuming.
Attachment is pervasive.
Attachment is invasive.
Attachment is corrosive.
Attachment is acidic.
Attachment is jealousy.
Attachment is suffocating.
Attachment is intoxicating.
Attachment is suffering.
Attachment is illusory.
Attachment is NOT LO♥E.
Attachment is DEATH.

Attachment is unnecessary.
AVOID *Attachment*.
ESCAPE *Attachment*.
BREAK FREE from *Attachment*.
RUN AWAY from *Attachment*.

"But I LO♥E you!"
"Whatever you do..."
"...DO NOT become attached!"
"Attachment KILLS LO♥E!"

"The Don"
10.07.2021

No Expectations

(Senza Aspettative)

No *hopes*.
No *dreams*.
No *plans*.
No *schemes*.
No *trajectory*.
No *path*.
No *road*.
No *journey*.
No *manipulations*.
No *preconceptions*.
No *certainty*.
No *purpose*.
No *destination*.
No *beginning*.
No *end*.
No *future*.
No *sadness*.
No *loss*.
No *happiness*.
No *excitations*.
No *sex*.
No *FUCKING*.
No *HATRED*.
No *LO♥E*.
No *HATE*.
No expectations.

"That's the way to BE!"
"That's the way to LIVE!"

"The Don"
10.07.2021

(Into) The Night

(Nella Notte)

The Night is the time I LO♥E.
The Night is the time I HATE.
The Night is good.
The Night is bad.
The Night can be beautiful.
The Night can be awful.
The Night, I never want to end.
The Night, I quickly want to end.
The Night, I want to last forever.
The Night, I want to be over now.
The Night is my friend.
The Night is my enemy.
The Night is my saviour.
The Night is my tormentor.
The Night is Freedom.
The Night is enslavement.
The Night is liberty.
The Night is imprisonment.
The Night is magical.
The Night is dull.
The Night is wonderful.
The Night is horrendous.
The Night is beautiful.
The Night is ugly.
The Night is Spiritual.
The Night is Heathen.
The Night is for LO♥ERS.
The Night is for SINNERS.
The Night is HEAVEN.
The Night is HELL.

Into The Night I go.
Into The Night I fall.
Into The Night I plunge.
Into The Night with hesitation.
Into The Night with DREAD.
Into The Night with FEAR.
Into the Night I LIVE.
Into The Night I DIE!

The Night will SAVE me.
The Night will KILL me!

"Who knows what The Night brings?"
"Are you ready?"
"Will it bring pleasure?"
"Or"
"Will It bring heartache?"

"The Don"
10.07.2021

In the Category of "Friend"
(Nella Categoria "Amico")

I am not your LO♥ER.
I'm not your *"man-bag"*.
I am not *"cuddly toy"*.
I'm not your *"sex toy"*.
I'm by your *"go-to"* boy.
I'm not your *"bit on the side"*.
I'm not your *"friend with benefits"*.
I'm not your *"fuck-buddy"*.
I'm not your *"boyfriend"*.
I'm in the category of friend.

You're not my *"bitch"*.
You're not my *"plaything"*.
You're not my *"sex thing"*.
You're not my *"mistress"*.
You're not my *"whore"*.
You're not my *"bit on the side"*.
You're not my *"friend with benefits"*.
You're not my *"fuck-buddy"*.
You're not my *"girlfriend"*.
I'm in the category of friend.

"The Don"
10.07.2021

I'm Writing the Script

(Sto Scrivendo la Sceneggiatura)

I have the narrative.
I have the plot.
I have the storyline.
I have the dialogue
I have the script.
Because...
... I'm writing the script.

I've written the final scene.
The hero gets the girl *(of course)*.
There's a happy end.
Everyone gets to go home.
No one is killed.
Everyone gets what they want.
Because...
... I'm writing the script.

It's a *"Rom-com"*.
It's a *musical*.
It's a *fantasy*.
It's a *"Gothic Tale"*.
It's a *"Moral Tale"*.
It's a *"Dickens"*.
It's a *"Baz Luhrmann"* classic.
It's a *"Quentin Tarantino"* homage.
It's a *"David Lynch"* masterpiece.
Because...
... I'm writing the script.

"I left John for you".
"He was so boring".
"He was putting me to sleep".
"So, I came over to your place to have some FUN!!!"

"The Don"
10.07.2021

ACCESS GRANTED

(Accesso Dato)

ACCESS GRANTED.
Permission is granted.
ACCESS GRANTED.
Entry permission is given.
ACCESS GRANTED.
Sufficient clearance.
ACCESS GRANTED.
Adequate level.
ACCESS GRANTED.
Appropriate grade.
ACCESS GRANTED.
Acceptable pay grade.
ACCESS GRANTED.
Non-Security risk.
ACCESS GRANTED.
Non-Suspicious character.
ACCESS GRANTED.
Training adequate.
ACCESS GRANTED.
Intellectually approved.
ACCESS GRANTED.
Visually non-impaired.
ACCESS GRANTED.
Vertically acceptable.
ACCESS GRANTED.
Mentally stable.
ACCESS GRANTED.
Sexually adequate.
ACCESS GRANTED.
Satisfies "slong" length requirements.
ACCESS GRANTED.
Hair length approved.
ACCESS GRANTED.
Personality acceptable.

Can I give you a cuddle?
ACCESS GRANTED.
Can I give you a hug?
ACCESS GRANTED.
Can I touch you knee?
ACCESS GRANTED.
Can I sit next to you?
ACCESS GRANTED.
Can I touch your feet?
ACCESS GRANTED.
Can I touch you down there?
ACCESS GRANTED.
Can I touch you anywhere?
ACCESS GRANTED.
Enter
ACCESS GRANTED.
System operating efficiently.
ACCESS GRANTED.
Correct code Entered.
ACCESS GRANTED.
Intruder allowed.
ACCESS GRANTED.
Alien.
ACCESS GRANTED.
ACCESS GRANTED.
ACCESS GRANTED.
ACCESS GRANTED.
ACCESS GRANTED.
ACCESS GRANTED.
ACCESS GRANTED.

"Just wishful thinking!"
"I'm a FANTACIST!"
"Access is still DENIED!"

"The Don"
28.06.2021

Books written by "The Don"

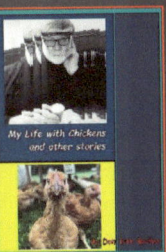

"My Life with Chickens & other stories: I Pity the Poor Immigrant"
Published:
10th September, 2019
Autobiography Book 1:
0 – 12 years old

"Poems for Misfits, Miscreants, Misanthropes, Mavericks, Losers & Malcontents!"
Published:
10th June, 2020
Book of Poems 1

"Poems for Troubled Minds & Trouble Hearts"
Published:
10th August, 2020
Book of Poems 2

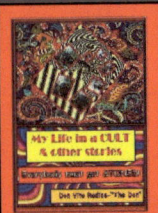

"My Life in a CULT & other stories: Everybody Must Get STONED!"
Published:
10th September, 2020
Autobiography Book 2:
15 – 30 years old

"Poems for Restless Minds & Restless Hearts"
Published:
10th October, 2020
Book of Poems 3

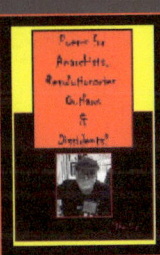

"Poems for Anarchists, Revolutionaries, Outlaws & Dissidents!"
Published:
10th November, 2020
Book of Poems 4

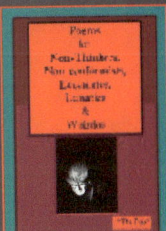

"Poems for Non-Thinkers & Eccentrics"
Published:
10th December, 2020
Book of Poems 5

"The Rantings of a Madman"
Published:
10th January, 2021
Book of Poems 6

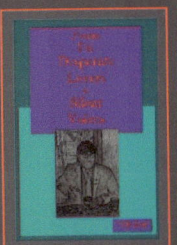

"Poems for Desperate Lovers & Silent Voices"
Published:
10th February, 2021
Book of Poems 7

"Poems for Tormented Minds & Tortured Souls"
Published:
10th March, 2021
Book of Poems 8

All available ONLY online

Books written by "The Don"

"Poems for ALIENS, Outsiders, Outcasts & other STRANGE BEINGS!"
Published: 10th April, 2021
Book of Poems 9

"Poems for Beings From Another Planet"
Published: 10th May, 2021
Book of Poems 10

"Poems for Mindless Beings & Lost Souls"
Published: 10th June, 2021
Book of Poems 11

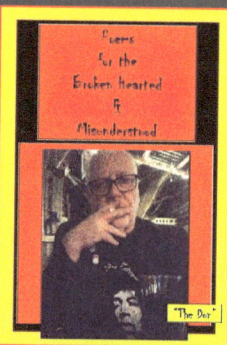

"Poems for the Broken Hearted & Misunderstood
Published: 10th July, 2021
Book of Poems 12

"Poems for Poems for the Bewildered, Dazed & Confused"
10th August, 2021
Book of Poems 13

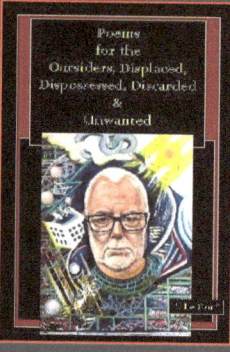

"Poems for the Outsiders, Displaced, Dispossessed, Discarded & Unwanted"
Published: 10th Sept, 2021
Book of Poems 14

All available ONLY online

"Poems for Secret Agents, Phantom Agents, Agents of Change, Agent Provocateurs & Agents of Chaos"
Published: 10th Oct, 2021
Book of Poems 15

Vito Radice ("The Don")
(Poet/Author/Polemicist/Non-Thinker/Non-Intellectual)
Email: vitoradice@gmail.com
Instagram: don_vito_radice
Facebook: Vito Radice
Mobile: +61490012461
(Australia)

www.ingramcontent.com/pod-product-compliance
Lightning Source LLC
Chambersburg PA
CBHW042048290426
44109CB00006B/145